How do I feel?

Written by Helen Dineen

Illustrated by Lucy Makuc

Collins

I am cross. This stiff jumper pricks my skin ...

but my blanket feels soft in my hand.

Ow! My ears throb ...

but I relax next to the tranquil river. Splash, splash!

Sniff, sniff! I think this spring
blossom stinks ...

but the damp soil in the park smells fresh.

Crunch! This sandwich has
a hard crust ...

but my plum is a
perfect snack. Squish!

Help! This light is too strong for me ...

but I like the crimson
spots on my lunchbox.

My little black cat Fluff understands
me best.

Fluff drinks her milk and I feel glad.

Map

After reading

Letters and Sounds: Phase 4

Word count: 100

Focus on adjacent consonants with short vowel phonemes, e.g. s/p/l/a/sh.

Common exception words: to, the, I, my, me, like, do, little

Curriculum links (EYFS): Understanding the World

Curriculum links (National Curriculum, Year 1): Science: Animals, including humans

Early learning goals: Reading: read and understand simple sentences; use phonic knowledge to decode regular words and read them aloud accurately; read some common irregular words; demonstrate understanding when talking with others about what they have read

National Curriculum learning objectives: Reading/word reading: read accurately by blending sounds in unfamiliar words containing GPCs that have been taught; Reading/comprehension: understand both the books they can already read accurately and fluently and those they listen to by checking that the text makes sense to them as they read, and correcting inaccurate reading

Developing fluency

- Encourage your child to follow the words as you read the first pages with expression.
- Take turns reading a page, encouraging your child to read with a tone to match the girl's feelings.

Phonic practice

- Practise reading words that contain adjacent consonants. Encourage your child to sound out and blend the following:

  milk   **spring**   **drinks**   **strong**

- Challenge your child to sound out the following words. Can they spot the word with three syllables?

  lunchbox   **sandwich**   **understands**   **blossom**

Extending vocabulary

- Ask your child to suggest an antonym for each of the following:

  pricks (e.g. *soothes, strokes*)   **tranquil** (e.g. *busy, noisy*)
  fresh (e.g. *stale, old*)   **hard** (e.g. *squashy*)